DISGRACEFUL
ARCHAEOLOGY
OR
THINGS YOU SHOULDN'T KNOW ABOUT
THE HISTORY OF MANKIND!

DISGRACEFUL
ARCHAEOLOGY

OR
THINGS YOU SHOULDN'T KNOW ABOUT
THE HISTORY OF MANKIND!

TEMPUS

First published 1999

PUBLISHED IN THE UNITED KINGDOM BY:

Tempus Publishing Ltd
The Mill, Brimscombe Port
Stroud, Gloucestershire GL5 2QG

PUBLISHED IN THE UNITED STATES OF AMERICA BY:

Tempus Publishing Inc.
2A Cumberland Street
Charleston, SC 29401

Tempus books are available in France, Germany and Belgium
from the following addresses:

Tempus Publishing Group	Tempus Publishing Group	Tempus Publishing Group
21 Avenue de la République	Gustav-Adolf-Straße 3	Place de L'Alma 4/5
37300 Joué-lès-Tours	99084 Erfurt	1200 Brussels
FRANCE	GERMANY	BELGIUM

British Library Cataloguing in Publication Data.
A catalogue record for this book is available from the British Library.

ISBN 0 7524 1476 3

Typesetting and origination by Tempus Publishing.
PRINTED AND BOUND IN GREAT BRITAIN.

CONTENTS

FOR PETER & GLYNIS BAHN, AND FOR HENRY CLEERE

FOREWORD

I was 12 years old when Archaeology first gripped and terrified me. It was the moment when the high priest of Amun, George Zukor in his fez and blazer, incanted the spell which enabled 3000-year-old Boris Karloff to push the lid off his sarcophagus and stagger away to throttle anyone wearing an archaeologist's uniform. From then on, any book featuring mummies was on my syllabus.

I didn't end up as an Egyptologist because everything on Sherlock Holmes, Wilson the Wonder Runner and War was also required reading, but I fancied myself as having a fair knowledge of Pharaohs. What a tremendous let down however when, decades later, my daughter, Sylvia, after taking tourists around the treasures of Egypt, told me about some of the more unusual practices in which the Kings indulged!

How was it that I didn't know that Seti masturbated for purposes other than fun? Gradually it seeped through to me that this fact and many others had been suppressed because, in the estimation of the great archaeologists, decent folk were not ready, and never would be, for such indecent revelations.

It was the old hypocrisy of censorship by prudery: fine for the wall-painting to show a Warrior King collecting mountains of foreskins from the fallen enemy, but absolutely forbidden to allow him to be seen exercising his own! I then began to speculate on what else had been locked away about prehistoric man, Egypt, the Maya, the Greeks, Romans and Chinese, etc; so I did a little probing, but the secrets were so well kept that only a professional would know where to dig. I called Paul Bahn, and this book was born.

Bill Tidy

At Khajuraho, India, the explicitly erotic subjects are presented with a liveliness and delicacy that deeply shocked the English colonial archaeologists who excavated the site in the early twentieth century. Guidebooks at that time discouraged visitors to the site for fear of impropriety and moral corruption,

INTRODUCTION

Archaeology is a bizarre pastime — it aims to reconstruct the past, to bring it back to life, by studying the objects and traces that have managed to survive years, centuries or millennia of decay or disturbance. Yet in the nineteenth century and the early part of our own, the picture of the past was carefully sanitised. There were endless learned books and papers devoted to the classification of objects, to the deeds and monuments of rulers, and to burials and treasures, but there was scant mention of a mass of equally fascinating aspects of ancient life, which would have served to flesh out the picture, made it more vivid and struck a chord with ordinary folk — the humorous, the scatological, and the sexual. Most of the silliness and bawdiness that helps make life worthwhile and which is such a vital part of being human was deliberately concealed or destroyed. Why?

In large measure this was due to prudishness and snobbery. It must have seemed beneath the dignity of learned scholars in the booklined groves of Academe to deal with such trivia — most of them were writing for their peers, after all, not for the great unwashed, and prudery was very much the norm through Victorian times and beyond. It resulted not only in cosmetic solutions such as the fig leaves placed over naughty bits of Classical statues, but also, at times, in outright obstruction. For example, 'cultured persons' are known to have destroyed many specimens of prehistoric Moche pottery from Peru depicting bestiality (primarily involving men and llamas) — which we know from sixteenth-century chroniclers was a widespread habit in highland Peru — out of misguided patriotism, in an effort to erase evidence of an abominable practice, and not wishing people to 'get the wrong idea' about their ancestors!

Other items are still being kept hidden — for example, the 'Turin Papyrus', a rare piece of sexually explicit imagery from ancient Egypt, is the most famous object in Turin's magnificent Museum of Egyptology, yet it is not on display — allegedly to prevent 'bambini' from seeing it — nor is any copy of it available at the museum in book, slide or postcard!

In general today the pendulum has swung the other way, and as archaeology becomes ever more popular the public is increasingly being given a picture of the past with 'warts and all'. Children, especially, love the scatological aspects of the past — such as multi-seated Roman toilets, or preserved turds — and it is no accident that the 'man using the cesspit' is the most popular bit of the Jorvik Viking Centre in York, as witnessed by the sale of its 'scratch and sniff' postcard ....

In putting this book together, therefore, we have unashamedly sought to put the spotlight on the more scurrilous or even shocking aspects of the past, the kind of material which would had Victorians reaching for the smelling salts or which would, until fairly recently, been published in passages of Latin or Greek to avoid shocking the uneducated!

Our brief was that we could be as obscene or politically incorrect as we wished, provided that everything we included was 'true'. Well, we cannot guarantee that it is all true, but we *can* assure readers that we have not made up anything at all — you could not make up things like this! Absolutely everything in this book has been published or recorded somewhere. Our title may lead some readers to imagine that we have drawn only on what many consider to be the main focus of archaeology, that is, the artifacts and ruins that have come down to us from the past. We have certainly done this where possible but, had we limited ourselves to such sources, the book would have been far slimmer and much more speculative as we tried to guess the uses of particular objects or rooms. But since, in fact, archaeology simply means the study of ancient things, or of the material traces of the human past, it follows that the invaluable writings that have survived from our ancestors, and especially those from the Classical world, can justifiably be included here — and we have drawn on them heavily for the unique insights they provide into aspects of their societies which otherwise would be lost for ever, or which would forever remain tantalisingly ambiguous in artistic depictions.

Archaeology is a vast, multi-faceted subject, with many roles to play, but one of its major functions, as the late Glyn Daniel often emphasised, is that of providing pleasure, whether through the simple joy of learning and discovery, the contemplation of beautiful images or objects, or the sheer fun of finding out that our ancestors were not always serious, downtrodden, spiritual and fearful creatures. They had a sense of humour, they were human beings like ourselves, and it diminishes their humanity to hide the kind of material presented here. Although it is all perfectly genuine, little of it has ever found its way into popular books before. It's time to pull off the fig leaves and take a long hard look at the *real* past.

Some may find this lowbrow little tome offensive. In reply, one can do no better than quote Captain John G. Bourke, the nineteenth-century American scholar whose amazing work of compilation was an invaluable source in preparing our book: 'As a physician, to be skilful, must study his patients both in sickness and in health, so the anthropologist must study man, not alone wherein he reflects the grandeur of his Maker, but likewise in his grosser and more animal propensities'. Or, to put it another way, one may cite a brief text that appeared in several early seventeenth-century books in Tuscany: 'Reader, if you find something that offends you in this most modest little book, don't be surprised. Because Divine, not human, is that which hath no blemish'.

On the other hand, to those readers who are not offended by this book's contents, may we make a plea for more material? We are sure that we have barely scratched the surface of this subject, and would greatly welcome suggestions for inclusion in future volumes ....

Paul Bahn

ACKNOWLEDGEMENTS

For their help in putting together this 'pot-pourri' (in every sense!), we would like to extend our warmest thanks to the following friends and colleagues Dave Evans, Bryan Sitch, Pete Sweeney, David Gill, Simon James, Steven Snape, Chris Edens, Carol Andrews, Karen Wise, Frank & A. J. Bock, Georgia Lee, Angelo Fossati, Gina Barnes, Bert Woodhouse, Kathy Cleghorn and Jan Wisseman-Christie. We would also like to thank Peter Kemmis Betty and all at Tempus Books for helping us to bring this disgraceful project to fruition.

REFERENCES

Bailey, M. 1991. Cupboard love: sex secrets of the British Museum. *The Observer*, 7 July, p. 7.

Barnes, G. D. 1984. *Kirkstall Abbey, 1147–1549: an historical study*. The Thoresby Society: Leeds.

Bourke, J. G. 1891. *Scatalogic Rites of all Nations. A dissertation upon the employment of excrementitious remedial agents in religion, therapeutics, divination, witchcraft, love-philters, etc, in all parts of the globe, based upon original notes and personal observation, and upon compilation from over one thousand authorities*. W. H. Lowdermilk & Co.: Washington D. C.

Cherici, P. 1995. *Celtic Sexuality. Power, Paradigms and Passion*. Duckworth: London.

Dover, K. J. 1978. *Greek Homosexuality*. Duckworth: London.

Faerman, M. *et al*. 1998. Determining the sex of infanticide victims from the late Roman era through Ancient DNA analysis. *Journal of Arch. Science* 25: 861-65.

Garland, R. 1995. *The Eye of the Beholder. Deformity and Disability in the Graeco-Roman World*. Duckworth: London.

Grant, M. & Mulas, A. 1982. *Eros in Pompeii. The Secret Rooms of the National Museum of Naples*. Bonanza Books: New York.

Kauffmann-Doig, F. 1979. *Sexual Behaviour in Ancient Peru*. Kompaktos: Lima.

Keuls, E. C. 1993. *The Reign of the Phallus. Sexual Politics in Ancient Athens*. Univ. of California Press: Berkeley.

Koman, K. 1995. Sexy words, raunchy pictures 1200 AD. *Harvard Magazine*, Sept/Oct, pp. 15-18.

Kuntz, T. 1998. At Harvard, a political sex scandal that's not news, but ancient history. *The New York Times*, October 18.

Lewin, R. 1999. *Merde: Excursions into scientific, cultural and socio-historical coprology*. Aurum Press: London.

Lister, A. M. 1997. Remedies for windy camels. *Nature* 390: 658-59.

Manniche, L. 1987. *Sexual Life in Ancient Egypt*. Routledge & Kegan Paul: London.

Mannix, D. P. 1960. *Those About to Die...* Panther Books: London.

Maulucci Vivolo, F. P. 1993. *Pompei. I Graffiti Figurati*. Bastogi Editrice Italiana: Foggia.

May, P. 1997. The oldest jokes of all. MAG *(Museums and Galleries)*, July/Aug.: p. 6.

McCall, A. 1979. *The Medieval Underworld*. Hamish Hamilton: London.

Miles, C. & Norwich, J. J. 1997. *Love in the Ancient World*. Weidenfeld & Nicolson: London.

Paludan, A. 1998. *Chronicle of the Chinese Emperors*. Thames & Hudson: London.

Paris, M. 1867. *English History*, vol III. (transl. J. A. Giles).

Pomeroy, S. B. 1975. *Goddesses, Whores, Wives and Slaves — Women in Classical Antiquity*. Schocken Books: New York.

Sabine, E. L. 1933. Butchering in Mediaeval London. *Speculum. A Journal of Medieval Studies* 8: 335-53.

Sabine, E. L. 1934. Latrines and cesspools of Mediaeval London. *Speculum. A Journal of Medieval Studies* 9: 303-21.

Salzmann, L. F. 1913. *Mediaeval Byways*. Constable: London.

Scarre, C. J. 1995. *Chronicle of the Roman Emperors*. Thames & Hudson: London.

Smith, H. 1998. World's first brothel unearthed. *The Guardian*, May 27.

Taylor, T. 1996. *The Prehistory of Sex, Four Million Years of Human Sexual Culture*. Fourth Estate: London.

Vallee, B. L. 1998. Alcohol in the Western World. *Scientific American* 278 (6): 62-67.

Wise, K., Clark, N. R. & Williams, S. R. 1994. A late Archaic period burial from the South-Central Andean coast. *Latin American Antiquity* 5 (3): 212-27.

Woodhouse, H. C. 1998. 'Medicine' on the rocks. *S. Afr. J. Ethnology* 21 (3): 206-7.

CENSORED!

Today some museum curators still keep archaeological material that they consider 'indecent' or inappropriate for public display under lock and key. Several important collections of Roman 'brothel tokens', small coinlike objects that depict the sexual service that has been paid for, currently lie, unpublished, in European museum basements. They convey more information than the simple existence of the different services in ancient times. At first glance, it might be hard to see why fellatio should be cheaper than vaginal intercourse from the rear, but a coin specialist from Warsaw has recently conducted a blind test on present-day prostitutes. He asked them what they charged for different positions and acts. Their scale corresponded precisely with the Roman scale. For prostitutes with many clients, one of the greatest hazards is vaginal soreness — hence deeply penetrating positions, such as sex from behind, are more painful and therefore cost more .... These tokens crossed language barriers, and prostitutes could see just what a man had paid for (1).

In 1819, the future king of Naples, Francis I, visited the Naples museum with his daughter to see the collections from Pompeii. He suggested to the curator that it would be better to restrict those items which dealt with erotic subjects to a single room, so that access could be limited to 'persons of mature age and of proven morality'. So 102 objects were isolated which might cause offence to the prevailing moral sentiments of the times, setting up the 'Gabinetto degli oggetti osceni'. In 1823, the name was changed to 'Gabinetto degli oggetti riservati', a euphemism. These works could only be shown to people who had a valid royal permit. In 1849, the doors were closed to everyone, after other nude sculptures and paintings had been added. Three years later, the entire collection was transferred to

a remote corner of the museum, as if to remove all trace of it. In 1860, Dumas père was made curator by Garibaldi, and he checked and catalogued the collection, renaming it 'Raccolta Pornografica', the same name it has today. More works were gradually put on show, and permission to see the special collection was granted to those who applied for a permit. Casual curiosity was thus discouraged.

The Roos Carr images are five small wooden human figures, dating to 2500 years ago, which were found in 1836 near the River Humber, in northern England. It has recently been found that what the Victorians took to be (and fitted as) detachable stubby arms are actually downward-curving penises!

For many years, unfounded reports circulated in whispers concerning the 'depraved habits' of the Incas and especially of the protagonists of the Moche culture — for example Posnansky, in 1925, referred to 'horrifying sexual pottery'. The fact that, years ago, museums did not show the 'erotic' pots led to legends such as 'homosexuality was then quite prevalent' — whereas in fact there are very few clear examples of it: there is one known depiction of homosexual anal intercourse surviving. However, early this century, a scholar mentioned the presence of ceramics with 'scenes of sodomy or pederasty', adding that 'a misunderstood modesty has led many collectors to destroy them'. No lesbianism is ever depicted. The sixteenth-century Spaniards were outraged by the widespread homosexuality and transvestism they found among the indigenous American peoples, and are thought to have systematically destroyed sculptures, jewellery and monuments that depicted and celebrated such practices.

Some nineteenth-century copies of rock paintings in Southern Africa deliberately omitted details such as urination or ejaculation coming from men and animals, and apparent infibulations.

Lots of primitive art in Java — some of it very phallic, from ancestor fertility cults — is hidden away in the back of museums.

Even in this century, little loin cloths or skirts were put on them in Djakarta's museums to spare the blushes of visitors — an ambassador's wife had complained!(2) One item, now in purdah in a cupboard in Djakarta museum, and not on display, is a fifteenth-century, 2m-high stone phallus with an inscription, from Candi Sukuh on Mt Lawu; the main shrine was surmounted by it. The upper part of the shaft is decorated with four spheres — possibly connected to the South-East Asian custom whereby little balls were inserted under the skin of the penis.

There is a Greek example of an illustration of a phallic statue on a potsherd from Cyrene. The published photo has the phallus blacked out (though it is clear on the actual potsherd). The excavator's wife insisted that the black pen be applied — she appears on a colour plate in the volume, planting flowers among the tombs!

Discovered during an era of sexual repression, 'pornographic' Greek vase paintings were, in many cases, locked away in secret museum cabinets — in Naples, Tarquinia, Munich, Boston, etc. As for ancient Egypt, a small fragment of a leather hanging from 1500 BC shows a girl playing the harp, while a naked man with a huge phallus turned backwards dances to the music — his left hand holds what seems to be a whip with several lashes. At the beginning of our century, the phallus was erased, and only an old photograph now shows it.

Indeed, whenever erotic drawings and figurines survived from Egypt, they frequently ended up in private collections or in inaccessible drawers in museums; and love and sex in the ancient Egyptian world are still known to only a few, because most of the texts were translated in the early twentieth century, when Victorian prudery was only just beginning to recede. Many of the Egyptian tomb reliefs and mythological stories were considered too shocking to publish. For example, an Egyptian creation legend describes how the god of creation, the sun god Atum, created himself from primordial matter. Then he was masturbated by the 'divine hand' and his seed formed the next two deities .... though in one papyrus a variant shows the god using his mouth instead of his hand. In the ancient daily rites for the god Atum at Karnak, the priestess of the temple reenacted this creation ritual with a large ithyphallic statue of Atum.

The Medieval and Later Antiquities section of the British Museum has a 'Museum Secretum', a locked cabinet, Cupboard 55, containing the collection of antiquities and objects of worship assembled by Dr Alfred Witt, a surgeon who made his fortune in Australia as a banker, and who was also a former mayor of Bedford, where he was famous for his Sunday morning lectures on this collection of phallic antiquities. He presented it to the Museum in 1865 'with the hope that some small room may be appointed for its reception', but the Victorians believed that this material — representations of the phallus from across the centuries and the continents — should not be exposed to

the female sex and young people, and placed it under lock and key. Ironically, of those who today apply to have the cupboard unlocked, 90 percent are women (3). There are Assyrian erect penises, Egyptian ones, Greek and Roman ones, medieval ones, phalluses with wings, with eyes, with hawks' heads, lead ones, phalluses in the form of signet rings, lamps, brooches .... Most were probably just symbols of good luck rather than anything overtly sexual.

The collection also contains a steel chastity belt — no such thing dating from the Middle Ages has ever been found, anywhere in the world, but the Victorians believed in them, so this is almost certainly a Victorian fabrication. In 1953, the British Library found some late eighteenth-century condoms which had been used as bookmarks in a 1783 *Guide to Health, Beauty, Riches and Honour*; they were made of sheep intestines with delicate pink drawstrings, and they too were deposited in Cupboard 55 (4).

Aesop's *Fables*, written 2600 years ago, far from being children's stories, were in fact coarse, violent and cruel. The Victorians translated them from the ancient Greek, but suppressed 100 of them, which have only recently appeared in English for the first time. The translators, Robert and Olivia Temple, say that 'the fables are not the pretty purveyors of Victorian morals that we have been led to believe. They are instead savage, coarse, brutal, lacking in all mercy or compassion. Some of them were probably suppressed because they were very violent and didn't suit the purposes of the Victorians. They were brutal or they were non-Christian. They were about alien gods; they contained coarse, peasant humour and were very rude.' Even some of the 250 or so that were already published had been mistranslated to give them a more comforting and more moral tone.

One example of an untranslated fable is about the beaver:

> A beaver's genitals serve, it is said, to cure certain ailments. So when the beaver is spotted and pursued to be mutilated — since he knows why he is being hunted — he will run for a certain distance, and he

BEAVER'S BALLS AND CAMEL SHIT PERMITS TO BE SHOWN ON DEMAND

5

will use the speed of his feet to remain intact. But when he sees himself about to be caught, he will bite off his own parts, throw them, and thus save his own life. The moral: is that wise men will, if attacked for their money, sacrifice it rather than lose their lives.

One, entitled 'The camel who shat in the river', goes as follows:

A camel was crossing a swiftly flowing river. He shat and immediately saw his own dung floating in front of him, carried by the rapidity of the current. 'What is that there?' he asked himself. 'That which was behind me I now see pass in front of me.' The moral: This applies to a situation where the rabble and the idiots hold sway, rather than the eminent and the sensible (5).

The asses appealing to Zeus:

> One day, the asses tired of suffering and carrying heavy burdens and they sent some representatives to Zeus, asking him to put a limit on their workload. Wanting to show them that this was impossible, Zeus told them that they would be delivered from their misery only when they could make a river from their piss. The asses took this reply seriously and, from that day until now, whenever they see ass piss anywhere they stop in their tracks to piss too. The moral: This fable shows that one can do nothing to change one's destiny.

The Hyenas:

> They say that hyenas change their sex each year and become males and females alternately. Now, one day a male hyena attempted an unnatural sex act with a female hyena. The female responded 'If you do that, friend, remember that what you do to me will soon be done to you.' The moral: This is what one could say to the judge concerning his successor, if he had to suffer some indignity from him.

The British Museum recently spent £1.8m on the Warren Cup, a Roman silver drinking cup from around AD 50, depicting two scenes, each set indoors: one of two males copulating on a mattress, the other of homosexual paedophilia. This is a rarity, because much of the homosexual imagery of the time was either hidden or destroyed.

WHAT A WAY TO GO!

Around 1260, 'at Tewkesbury, a Jew fell into a privy, and out of respect for his sabbath, on which day the accident happened, would not allow himself to be extricated till the following day, which was Sunday; and in consequence he died, being suffocated by the foul stench.'

In early imperial times, a very nasty Roman gentleman pushed his long-suffering slaves too far, and they decided to murder him in the bathhouse by shoving the sponge-stick (used for wiping the backside) down his throat — presumably to leave no trace of cause of death, as well as to really stick it to him. When he stopped kicking, they threw him down on the burning-hot floor to make sure he was dead. Unfortunately he recovered consciousness and lived long enough to see them suitably punished ....

In 1326 in England, Richard the Raker was drowned — he entered a privy, seated himself, and the rotten planks of the floor gave way, letting him fall into the deep cesspool filth. There his body was found by a fellow raker.

Another fatal accident occurred in Bread Street Ward: in the courtyard of a house, two men had dug a privy well to the depth of five casks — they had cribbed it with a pile of five casks in which new wine had been kept. As one of the boards from the end of one of the casks had fallen to the bottom of the well, one of the men put down a ladder and began to descend, but was overcome by fumes (carbon dioxide) from the wine-soaked staves, and dropped unconscious to the bottom. The other man descended to rescue him, but he too fell unconscious, and both were asphyxiated!

The Roman emperor Caracalla (AD 211–170) was suffering from a stomach upset on a journey, and ordered a halt while he went to relieve himself — only a single attendant went with him. The rest of the bodyguard turned their backs in respect for the emperor's privacy. One officer of the bodyguard killed him with a single sword thrust as he was lowering his breeches (6).

The Roman emperor Elagabalus (AD 204-22) was hacked to death by the praetorian guard as he sat on the lavatory, and his body thrown down a sewer. In life, he used to liked to surprise guests with rare dishes — sometimes he would serve exact replicas of the food he was eating, but in wood, ivory, pottery or stone. The guests were expected to continue eating as though nothing had happened.

7

In England, the Saxon king Edmund Ironside was assassinated while seated on a wooden lavatory — someone hiding in the pit below thrust his longsword up his backside into his bowels, killing him instantly (7).

Sir Arthur Aston, a Royalist commander during the English Civil war, was beaten to death with his own wooden leg by Cromwell's men (**8**).

TRY THIS FOR THIGHS!

Among the Ancient Greeks, as depicted on vases, male homosexuals did indulge in anal intercourse, but they also often rubbed the penis back and forth between the young man's thighs — this is known as intercrural intercourse.

Straton, a Greek physicist of the 3rd century BC, compared girls unfavourably with boys: 'They're all so dull from behind, and the main thing is, you've nowhere to put a roaming hand'.

Dioskorides, a Greek doctor of the first century AD, recommends a friend to 'delight in the rosy bum' of his wife when she is pregnant, treating her as a 'male Aphrodite', and Rhianos rapturously talks of the 'glorious bum' of a boy, so beautiful that even old men itch for it.

The fifth/fourth century BC Greek playwright Aristophanes, in *Birds*, has a character say 'Where the father of a good-looking boy will meet me and go on at me as if I'd done him a wrong:

> That was a nice way to treat my son, Stilbonides! You met him when he'd had a bath, leaving the gymnasium, and you didn't kiss him... you didn't say a word to him, you didn't pull him close to you, you didn't tickle his balls — and you an old friend of the family!

And in *Knights*, the Sausage-Seller says '..here's a folding stool for you, and a boy (he's no eunuch) who'll carry it for you. And if you feel like it sometimes, make a folding-stool of him!'.

Greek vases often show old men fingering the genitals of young men. In the play *Clouds* by Aristophanes, it is recalled that when

boys 'were sitting in the trainer's, they had to put one thigh
forward in order not to show anything cruel to those outside.
Then, when a boy got up again, he had to brush the sand
together and take care not to leave an imprint of his youth' for
the old men to look at. This means that the sight of the boys'
genitals would torment the spectators, while the old men might
brood longingly over the mark in the sand where the genitals
had rested (**9**).

It was said that Julius Caesar had been King Nicomedes's
catamite — and this was frequently quoted by his enemies. For
example, Licinius Calvus wrote 'The riches of Bithynia's King
Who Caesar on his couch abused', while Dolabella called him
'the Queen's rival and inner partner of the royal bed', and Curio
the Elder 'Nicomedes's Bithynian brothel'. Bibulus, Caesar's
colleague in the consulship, called him 'the Queen of Bithynia'.
When his own soldiers followed his decorated chariot in the

Gallic triumph, they chanted ribald songs, as they were privileged to do (**10**):

> Home we bring our bald whoremonger
> Romans, lock your wives away!
> All the bags of gold you lent him
> Went his Gallic whores to pay.'

Caesar also had numerous and extravagant affairs with women, including several queens, and was called 'every woman's husband and every man's wife'.

Mark Antony alleged that Julius Caesar made Octavian (Augustus) submit to unnatural relations as the price of adoption; Octavian was also said to have sold his favours to the

Governor-General of Spain for 3000 gold pieces, and it was claimed that he used to soften the hair on his legs by singeing them with red-hot walnut shells.

Once, while sacrificing, the emperor Tiberius (42 BC–AD 37) took an erotic fancy to the acolyte who carried the incense casket, and could hardly wait for the ceremony to end before hurrying him and his brother, the sacred trumpeter, out of the temple and indecently assaulting them both. When they protested at this, he had their legs broken.

The emperor Caligula persistently teased Cassius Charea, who was no longer young, for his supposed effeminacy. Whenever he demanded the watchword, Caligula used to give him 'Priapus' or 'Venus'; and if he came to acknowledge a favour, always stuck out his middle finger for him to kiss, and waggled it obscenely.

Aristophanes' comedy is rich in obscene and scatological invective, and abounds in abusive terms alluding to anal sex — 'Wide-assed' (*euryproktos*) was a common insult that he expanded into'with gaping ass hole' (*chaunoproktos*). The politician Cleisthenes was evidently known as a passive homosexual, and Aristophanes never tired of making fun of his effeminate ways and his hospitable rear end.

The concept of anal penetration as demeaning and humiliating is perhaps best seen in what may be termed the 'radish treatment' (see below, p.88).

One Greek vase shows a Persian captive about to submit to anal penetration by a Greek.

Eubolos, a comic poet of the fourth century, said of the Greeks who spent ten long years in capturing Troy: 'No one ever set eyes on a single *hetaira* (harlot); they wanked themselves for ten years. It was a poor sort of campaign for the capture of one city, they went home with arses much wider than the gates of the city that they took.' (11)

WITH FRIENDS LIKE THESE, WHO NEEDS ENEMAS?

Louis XIV is said to have endured more than 2000 enemas during his reign, often meeting with various dignitaries during the procedure, which clearly made him public enema No. 1. (**12**)

The Late Classic Maya (AD 600-900) may have ritually used hallucinogenic enemas (probably made of mead, tobacco juice, mushrooms and morning glory seeds) to go into a trance state more quickly than through oral consumption. Some are illustrated on their pottery, while certain mysterious artifacts such as slim bone tubes found in graves may also be linked with the practice. Similarly, a prehistoric tomb on the south coast of Peru, dating to 3000–1000 BC, contains a 45-year old man, buried with various artifacts including what is thought to be an

enema apparatus used for hallucinogens or other substances.

A rock painting in South Africa's Free State Province seems to depict the administration of an enema. A figure bends forward with buttocks raised and hands on the ground. A second figure approaches from the right to administer the enema, apparently using a horn fitted with a plunger. The apprehensive patient raises one leg in the air in anticipation of some discomfort. There are two onlookers.

The ancient Egyptians had highly developed medical knowledge — one palace official rejoiced in the title Keeper of the Royal Rectum for his knowledge of enemas (13).

The Roman emperor Claudius (ruled AD 41–54) was murdered by being fed poisoned mushrooms — one version is that he fell into a coma but vomited up the entire contents of his stomach and was then poisoned a second time, either by a gruel — the excuse being that he needed food to revive him — or by means of an enema, the excuse being that his bowels must be emptied too.

FRIENDS, ROMANS........BAAAARF

Mark Antony, according to Plutarch (the Greek historian of the first century AD), was hated for his drunkenness, his gross intrigues with women, and the many days spent sleeping off his debauches, wandering about with an aching head and befuddled wits, and his many nights spent in revels. The story goes that he once attended a banquet given for the wedding of Hippias the actor; he ate and drank all night, and then, when he was summoned to attend a political meeting early in the morning at the Forum, he appeared in public surfeited with food and vomited into his toga, which one of his friends held ready for him (**14**).

Similarly, the emperor Claudius was always ready for food and drink — it was seldom that he left a dining hall except gorged and sodden; he would then go to bed and sleep supine with his mouth wide open, thus allowing a feather to be put down his throat, which would bring up the superfluous food and drink as vomit.

From ancient Egypt there is a depiction in tomb 49 at Thebes of a woman (presumably hung-over) throwing up, while there is also a Greek vase showing a young harlot comforting a vomiting customer.

UNDERNEATH THE ARCHES...

In ancient Rome, some prostitutes did not have the security of a brothel in which to work, but instead practised their trade out of doors under archways — the word 'fornicate' is actually derived from the Latin word for 'arch' (*fornix*). (**15**)

In Kingston-upon-Hull, in northern England, the medieval council's attitude to prostitution was ambivalent. The corporation was prepared in the 1490s to let out the town walls and towers and the foreland to the whores, receiving £3-£8 a year in rent.

Among the Greek words for 'harlot' a common one is '*chamaitype*', 'earth-striker', which shows that they often worked on the ground.

BROTHELS AND BATHS

The term 'brothel' comes from the Old English word for wretch, perhaps referring to the living conditions of the women who worked in the early houses of prostitution. In the medieval period, lower-class women could avoid a life of toil and drudgery by bartering their sexuality, despite the risk of disease; while nuns and married upper-class women could escape the confines of their life by secretly entering a brothel. As long as they profited from the brothels, the nobles and clergy turned a blind eye to the houses devoted to sexual adventure, and indeed were often to be found among the clientele.

At Ashkelon, Israel, the Roman (fourth century) bathhouse contained lamps decorated with erotic images, while a Greek inscription 'Enter, enjoy and ....' suggests the bathhouse served as a brothel. It was probably in the red light district — an earlier Roman villa on the site had a room full of lamps decorated with erotic images. As mixed bathing came into vogue in Claudius's reign, bath houses became like bordellos — in fact one author from Nero's time wrote of a father who went to the baths, leaving one child at home, only to return from the baths a prospective father of two more. The poet Martial (first century AD) wrote 'The bathman lets you among the tomb-haunting whores only after putting out his lantern'.

Ancient Egypt, on the other hand, has its 'Bes chambers' — early this century archaeologists at Saqqara uncovered four rooms of a mud-brick house; some had brick benches along the walls, and the walls were decorated with representations of the god Bes, 1-1.5 m high, covered with stucco and painted. The dwarf god Bes was often present where physical love is celebrated. In addition, 32 phallic figures were recovered from the debris. So these 'Bes chambers' may have been for lady inmates and their clients, or a place of worship linked to procreation.

The names of medieval brothel areas were often explicit, and some still survive in contracted form: in fourteenth century London there were Slut's Hole, Gropecuntlane (now Grape Lane), and Codpiece Alley (now Coppice Alley). Outside the city walls was Cokkeslane. In Paris there was rue Trousse-Puteyne (Whore's Slit Street) — Mary Stuart is said to have fainted whenever her route took her through there. There was also a rue Grattecon (Scratchcunt street), and rue du Poil au Con (now rue Pélécan), where there were prostitutes who refused to comply with a city regulation requiring them to shave their privates. (16)

A 2000-year-old brothel has recently been unearthed at Salonika in Greece — all kinds of sex toys were found inside, including a small clay dildo, several erotic figurines, and a red pitcher with a phallic spout. There were also innumerable offerings to Aphrodite, the goddess of love. The room containing this material of the 1st century BC conveniently bordered a bath house.

At Pompeii, sometimes taverns had rooms for prostitution upstairs, where the names of waitresses and prostitutes are found scribbled on walls. The graffiti refer to the women's vices and attractions, and announce that some women can be had for two 'as' — the price of a loaf of bread. But these may be written as insults, rather than reflect a true price. The highest price of a woman is given as 16 as.

Strabo, the Greek geographer of the first century BC, said Corinth had more than 1000 prostitutes; he tells of a Corinthian courtesan who was reproached for being lazy and refusing to do wool working. In her bawdy reply, she punned on the word 'histos' which can refer to anything erectable, including a loom: 'Such as I am, in this short time I have taken down three looms [erections] already'.

A fragment by the fourth-century playwright Alexis of Thurii provides a catalogue of tricks whereby an artful madam prepares her novice slave prostitutes for business, including elevator

17

shoes and false buttocks to satisfy customers who were partial to women's rear ends. They must also have charming manners: 'Does she have healthy teeth? By force she's kept laughing, so that the customers see what a dainty mouth she has. If she doesn't like to laugh, she must spend the day indoors, with a twig of myrrh upright between her lips, just like the goats' heads displayed in this way at the butcher shops so that the customers will buy them. That way in time she smiles whether she likes it or not.'

Prostitutes in the ancient port of Ephesus wore sandals with reversed lettering on the sole, so they stamped 'Follow me' on the sand as they walked. A carved stone footprint of this kind can be seen in the city ruins. (**17**)

In the entrance hall of a Pompeii brothel is a painting of a man holding a double penis, maybe one for action and one for luck. Pompeii had 12,000 inhabitants and 34 brothels. One Roman word for a prostitute was 'Nonaria' — ninth hour — which, as they counted time from dawn, meant 4 pm, the time when brothels opened. One painting of sex in a Pompeii brothel has '*Lente Impelle*' written above it, 'Push Slowly' (**18**).

MISOGYNISTS

According to Herodotus, the Greek historian of the fifth century BC, the women of ancient Egypt were all unfaithful. When a son of Ramesses II had been blind for 10 years, an oracle from the city of Buto declared to him that the time of his punishment was drawing to an end, and that he should regain his sight by washing his eyes with the menses of a woman who had never had intercourse with any man but her own husband. Pheros made a trial with his own wife first, but still remained blind, even though he tried with all women, one after the other. When he finally recovered his sight, he took all the women whom he had tried, gathered them in one town, and burnt them and the town — but he married the woman by whose means he had recovered sight.

In a Mesopotamian Cuneiform wedding contract testimony, arguing about the return of the house as part of the dowry, Iddin-aba backs out, saying 'Your daughter I shall not marry. Tie her up and throw her in the river' (a reference to the river trial of truth-telling).

An Egyptian papyrus in the British Museum, 'The Instruction of Ankhsheshonq', contains rules written by a priest for his youngest son — including the following:

> He who sends spittle up to the sky will have it fall on him;
> Let your wife see your wealth — do not trust her with it;
> Do not open your heart to your wife — what you have said to her goes to the street;
> Instructing a woman is like having a sack of sand whose side is split open;
> When a man smells of myrrh, his wife is a cat before him;
> Do not laugh at a cat.

Hesiod, a Greek poet of the eighth century BC, was very anti-women, seeing them as a necessity but an economic liability with vices: 'Do not let a woman with a sexy rump deceive you with wheedling and coaxing words; she is after your barn. The man who trusts a woman trusts deceivers.'

Semonides, a poet-philosopher of the seventh century BC, compared women to different creatures: (19)

> From the beginning the god made the mind of woman
> A thing apart. One he made from the long-haired sow;
> While she wallows in the mud and rolls about on the ground,
> Everything at home lies in a mess.
> Another doesn't take baths but sits about
> In the shit in dirty clothes and gets fatter and fatter ....
> The next one was made from a dog, nimble, a bitch like its mother,
> And she wants to be in on everything that's said or done.
> Scampering about and nosing into everything,
> She yaps it out even if there's noone to listen.
> Her husband can't stop her with threats,
> Not if he flies into a rage and knocks her teeth out with a rock ....
> Another woman is from the stumbling and obstinate donkey,
> Who only with difficulty and with the use of threats
> Is compelled to agree to the perfectly acceptable thing
> She had resisted. Otherwise in a corner of the house
> She sits munching away all night long, and all day long she sits munching at the hearth
> Even so she'll welcome any male friend
> Who comes around with sex on his mind.
> Another kind of woman is the wretched, miserable tribe that comes from the weasel.
> As far as she is concerned, there is nothing lovely or pleasant
> Or delightful or desirable in her.
> She's wild over love-making in bed,

19

But her husband wants to vomit when he comes near her
....
Another one is from the monkey. In this case Zeus has outdone himself
In giving husbands the worst kind of evil.
She has the ugliest face imaginable; and such a woman
Is the laughingstock throughout the town for everyone.
Her body moves awkwardly all the way up to its short neck;
She hardly has an ass and her legs are skinny. What a poor wretch is the husband
Who has to put his arm round such a mess!

There are even traces of prehistoric violence to women. A prehistoric skeleton from South Africa, dating to within the last 2000 years, is that of an adult woman who was shot at close range by two arrows in the back. And the oldest evidence of interhuman violence, recently published, is the skeleton of an adult female from the late Ice Age with an arrowhead in her pelvis — and she was in Sicily! Perhaps a horse's skull was found with her ....

ANIMAL LOVERS

From the sixteenth century, chroniclers like Cieza and others refer to clear cases of zoophilia as practised by the natives of Peru the habit of copulating with llamas seems to have been a widespread habit among the natives of the Andes. Early in the twentieth century there were pottery pieces, representing cases of coupling with llamas, in museums and collections in Lima, but they were destroyed by 'cultured' persons' due to a mistaken patriotism, in an effort to erase proofs that showed the presence of a practice considered abominable.' They have been systematically destroyed (20). The Incas were said to have collected pornographic Moche pottery.

Herodotus was shocked by the sexual relations between men and animals in Egypt — he says a woman had open intercourse with a he-goat; this was probably a ritual act, as when the virility of the Apis bull was strengthened by women showing their privates to it.

In the dream books, there are various combinations of animals and people — men may copulate with jerboas, swallows and pigs, while women have a choice between mouse, horse, donkey, ram, wolf, lion, crocodile, snake, baboon, ibis or falcon. One Egyptian curse was 'May a donkey copulate with your wife and children'.

According to Meleagros, 'female eros' now finds favour with him, and 'the squeeze of a hairy arse' he leaves to 'herdsmen who mount their goats'.

In the Graeco-Roman world, 'Satyrs' were ugly, earthy, drunken creatures; they masturbated constantly if no living being with a suitable orifice was available, but they preferred mules, horses or deer and even the neck of a jar might be pressed into service. One Greek vase shows a satyr about to mount an unsuspecting sphinx from the rear!

In the Roman games and shows, sexual relations between a woman and an animal were often exhibited 'under the stands', and occasionally in the arena, but the trouble was in finding an animal that would perform on schedule. A jackass or even a large dog that would voluntarily mount a woman before a screaming mob was rare, and of course the woman was forced to cooperate — a willing woman destroyed most of the crowd's fun. With a bull or giraffe, the victim usually didn't survive the ordeal; they would use old women from the provinces who didn't fully realize what the job entailed until it was too late.

Apuleius, a Roman writer of the second century AD, tells of one woman who had poisoned five people to get their property; she was sentenced to be thrown to the wild beasts in the arena, but first, as additional punishment and disgrace, she was to be raped by a jackass. A bed was set up in the middle of the arena, inlaid with tortoise shell and provided with a feather mattress and an embroidered Chinese bedspread. She was tied spread-eagled on the bed. The jackass had been trained to kneel on the bed, otherwise the business could not have been concluded successfully. When the show was over, wild beasts were turned loose in the arena and quickly put an end to the wretched woman's suffering.

Apuleius also tells of a wealthy noblewoman who asked a trainer to bring one of his trained jackasses to her room at night, promising him a fabulous sum of money. She made elaborate preparations — four eunuchs placed a feather bed on the floor, with soft pillows at one end. She ordered the trainer to lead the jackass to the bed, get him to lie down, and then she rubbed him with oil of balsam. Then the trainer was told to leave and return the next morning. She demanded the jackass's services so often that the trainer was afraid she might kill herself, but after a few weeks his only concern was that she might totally exhaust the valuable animal.

Mythology saw some hybrid monsters as the product of a union between a mortal woman and an animal, as in the famous story of Pasiphaë, the wife of Minos king of Crete, who became enamoured of a bull. In lovesick despair at her failure to achieve congress with the object of her passion, Pasiphaë sought the help

21

of the famed craftsman Daidalus, who manufactured a marvellously lifelike heifer, inside which the queen then hid. The unholy coupling took place, in consequence of which Pasiphaë gave birth to the Minotaur...... **(21)**

The first discoveries of rock art in the Sahara were made in 1847 by two soldiers (Dr François Félix Jacquot and Captain Kook of the Foreign Legion), part of General Cavaignac's expedition against the Ksour tribes. Jacquot published two engravings of rock figures ('a family out hunting' and 'a warrior's lesson to his son') but noted that others were of appalling indecency which would prevent them ever emerging from his files (**22**):

> One can see, in full view and with no secrecy, the unnatural intercourse that brought the storm of fire down on the cities whose names you know well; a

hideous coupling.....the strange perversion of desire which, according to Theocritus, brought together the shepherds of Sicily and their goats, also has its analogues at Thyout, only here that peaceful animal is replaced by the lion.

There are lots of other depictions of bestiality in prehistoric art — our favourite is the Italian petroglyph at Naquane, Valcamonica, showing a man buggering some poor animal while waving happily to the viewer!

REAL PERVERTS

Herodotus claimed that in Egypt the wives of notable men, and women of great beauty and reputation, were not given to the embalmers immediately, but only after they had been dead for three or four days, so the embalmers could not have carnal intercourse with them — one was found doing it with a newly dead woman, and was denounced by his fellow workmen. Xenophon of Ephesus says that a man kept the embalmed body of his wife in his bedroom... we don't know why.

The Roman emperor Tiberius was invited to dinner by Cestius Gallus, a lecherous old spendthrift, and he accepted on condition that the waitresses should be naked. On retiring to Capri, Tiberius made himself a private sporting house where sexual extravagances were practised for his secret pleasure. Bevies of girls and young men, whom he had collected from all over the Empire as adepts in unnatural practices, would perform before him in groups of three to excite his waning passions. A number of small rooms were furnished with the most indecent pictures and statuary obtainable .... and erotic manuals from Egypt. He had nooks of lechery in the woods and glades of the island, and had boys and girls dressed up as Pans and nymphs.

An ingenious torture devised by Tiberius was to trick men into drinking huge draughts of wine, and then suddenly to knot a cord tightly around their genitals, which not only cut into the flesh but prevented them from urinating.

Similarly, the emperor Nero (AD 37–68) invented a novel game he was released from a den dressed in the skins of wild animals, and attacked the private parts of men and women who stood bound to stakes. And after working up sufficient excitement he was screwed by his freedman Doryphorus, who later married him — on the wedding night he imitated the screams and moans of a girl being deflowered.

According to a papyrus in Berlin, King Sneferu of Egypt got bored, and asked his chief magician Djadjamankh what he should do. The magician suggested he go to the palace lake, order a boat, and call for some young girls from his palace — watching them row up and down would cheer him up. He ordered twenty women with beautiful limbs and breasts and braids, twenty young women who had not borne children. And twenty fish nets as well. 'Let the nets be draped on the women, when they have taken their clothes off.' (23)

At the beginning of his reign, Domitian would spend hours alone every day catching flies, and stabbing them with a needle-sharp pen.

The Greek sculptor Praxiteles (fourth century BC) carved a nude Aphrodite, using his mistress Phryne, a famous *hetaira* (courtesan), as the model .... Pliny relates that one man became

so enamoured that he embraced the statue during the night and left a stain on it....

(Phryne, incidentally, became enormously rich, as Praxiteles was not her only lover. On one occasion she was charged with profane behaviour and put on trial: defending her was another of her lovers, the orator Hyperides. Seeing that he was making no progress in the case he suddenly decided to take a completely different line of defence so he pulled down her dress, revealing a pair of perfect breasts. Confronted by such beauty, the judges could only acquit her — though a new law was passed immediately afterwards, forbidding the accused to be present in court while the verdict was under consideration ....] **(24)**

Elagabalus, the Syrian-born emperor of Rome (AD 218–22), was bisexual and a transvestite. He would frequent taverns at night, wearing a wig, and there ply the trade of a female huckster. He also frequented the notorious brothels, drove out the prostitutes

55

and played the prostitute himself. He 'married' a slave who was allowed to beat him like a wife. He also wished to be transformed into a woman, and asked physicians to contrive a woman's vagina in his body by means of an incision, and promised them large sums for doing so. Another story tells of his delight in a man with peculiarly large private parts, but he lost interest when this man was unable to perform in bed.

BOOZE

An ancient Egyptian verse:

> When I embrace her
> and her arms are open,
> I feel like a man in incense land
> who is immersed in scent.
> When I kiss her
> and her lips are open
> I rejoice
> without even having drunk beer.

An Egyptian papyrus of the nineteenth Dynasty say: 'Beer robs you of all human respect, it affects your mind, and here you are like a broken rudder, good for nothing.'

There is also an Egyptian fragment of limestone with a drawing on it depicting a king with five-o'clock shadow; In a tomb at Elkab, there is a picture of a high-born woman at a party saying 'Give me eighteen jugs of wine — I want to get drunk, my insides are as dry as straw'. A painting from Khety's Tomb, c.2100 BC, even shows guests being carried away from a banquet after drinking too much wine.

In a newly-discovered letter from the Roman fort of Vindolanda, in northern England, a commander of a cavalry section wrote to his prefect: 'The lads have no beer — please send some'.

25

'I DID NOT HAVE SEX WITH THAT WOMAN...'

In 1400 BC, there was a political scandal in Mesopotamia — the Semitic Museum of Harvard University has cuneiform tablets showing a corruption and sex investigation. Unearthed in northern Iraq in the 1920s, they record a judicial panel's impeachment proceedings against Mayor Kushshiharbe of Nuzi. Dogged by an aggressive prosecution, a political leader denies an illicit affair — 'I did not have sex with her', although one of his assistants swears to it. The Mayor was accused of taking bribes (one maid, one complete oxhide and wood for two yokes), and abducting people for ransom (two shekels of gold, one ox and two male sheep), and stealing. He even expropriated manure to fertilize his gardens — Mar-Ishtar, a farmer, said: 'The manure for [one plot] of land the gardener of Kushshiharbe took away from me. So I said "Why did you take away my manure?", and he said "As for you, the mayor has ordered you to be flogged".' The mayor was accused of committing adultery with a woman named Humerelli — he vehemently denied the charge, but one of his agents, Ziliptilla, said it was true: 'We brought her to the place of Kushshiharbe, and he had sex with her'. The mayor said: 'No! Emphatically no! Not a word of it is true, I did not have sex with her!' A second man, Paleya, said: 'I called to Humerelli and took her over to the brothel of Tilunnaya, and Kushshiharbe had sex with her.' The mayor said 'May I perish if Palteya did bring Humerelli over to the brothel of Tilunnaya that I might have sex with her.' He was also accused of adorning his private home with a gate fashioned from 30-40 pieces of wood taken from the palace gate. The records of the final verdict in the case have never been found ... (25)

WIND-BREAKS — OR GONE WITH THE WIND

The historian Suetonius (AD 69–140) said of the emperor Claudius that he intended to publish an edict allowing to all people the liberty of giving vent at table to any distension caused by flatulence. This was upon hearing of a person whose modesty, under such circumstances, had nearly cost him his life.

The obscene tenures by which certain estates in England were held in 'sergeantcy' date back at least to the early fourteenth century: Baldwin le Petteur (note the name) held 110 acres of land in Hemington, County of Suffolk, by sergeantcy, for which on Christmas Day, every year, before our sovereign lord the King of England, he had to perform one saltus, one sufflatus and one bumbulus (or pettus) — i.e. he was to dance, make a noise with his cheeks, and let a fart. As Camden says in his *Britannia*: 'Such was the plain, jolly mirth of those days'. (26)

Similarly, at Montluçon in France, any prostitute who was about to enter the town for the first time had to pay a toll on the bridge of one fart. According to Victor Hugo, this custom was generally known in France in the fifteenth century, and records of the Montluçon toll system go back to 1398. In England, the stage directions to old Morality Plays often include 'Here Satan letteth a fart'. Later, a poem was written called 'The fart censured in the Parliament House', based on an 'escape' of this kind that took place in 1607, though possibly it occurred in Elizabethan times. (27)

The fart was a divinity among the ancient Egyptians, the personification of a natural function. It was depicted as a crouching child making some effort. The ancient Pelusians, a people of lower Egypt, venerated a Fart, which they worshipped

under the symbol of a swelled paunch. Farts were a good omen for the Greeks, a bad one for the Romans.

The deities of many ancient peoples — Greeks, Romans, Egyptians and others — were restricted in their powers and functions. They were not able to cure all diseases, only particular kinds, each god being a specialist; consequently, each was supposed to take charge of a section of the human body. Hence, Bel-Phegor (see below, p. 75) was doubtless the deity to whom the devotee resorted for the alleviation of ailments connected with the rectum and belly — the worshipper would offer him the sacrifice of flatulence and excrement, testimonies of the good health for which gratitude was due to the deity. In medieval times, they were replaced by Saints — for example, Saint Erasmus was in charge of 'the belly with the entrayles', while Saint Phiacre was invoked to relieve people of 'the phy or emeroids, of those especially which grow in the fundament'.

Although the adoration of Flatulence cannot be found among the Chinese, religious customs equally revolting have been ascribed to them. Mohammedans who travelled through China in the ninth century reported that 'the Chinese are addicted to the abominable vice of Sodomy, and the filthy practice of it they number among the indifferent things they perform in honor of their idols'.

There is a story that Henry VIII of England enjoyed rhyming, and one day, while travelling on the river from Westminster to Greenwich to visit 'a fair lady whom he loved and lodged in the tower of the park', he challenged Sir Andrew Flamock to compose with him. The King wrote:

> Within this tower
> There lieth a flower
> That hath my heart.

Exactly what Sir Andrew replied has been kept discreetly hidden, but a version of his answer appeared in one of the worst plays of almost any century:

> Within this hour
> She pist full sower
> And let a fart

Legend has it that the monarch was not amused and bid Flamock 'avant varlet and begone'. (28)

MALE BITS AND HOW TO USE THEM

Male sexual organs are depicted in Moche pottery, showing testicles and penis, with the foreskin folded back showing the gland. These were drunk from, thus converting them into a sort of instrument of artificial fellatio.

One Moche pot shows a male anally penetrating a female asleep in bed between her parents.

In Moche pottery, 95 percent of the sex depicted seems to be anal, though heterosexual; the fellatio is all heterosexual, but there is no cunnilingus. Whether engaged in vaginal, anal or oral intercourse, the male face always remains totally impassive.

Musical instruments can often be seen in an erotic context, especially in Graeco-Roman figurines where the man's phallus is either part of the musical instrument or used for playing it.

The Romans had 'willy pots' — the Roman site of Stonea Grange in Britain produced a pot with no less than 21 phalli shown on it. In fact the Romans were obsessed with phalli — little boys wore them round the neck, there were phalli hung up in Pompeian houses with bells on them and wings; they had phalli outside the doors, on street corners, etc. Many other ancient cultures, such as the Egyptian, also employed erotic amulets with huge phalli.

The House of the Vettii at Pompeii has a fountain in the form of an ithyphallic figure, with its phallus serving as a waterspout; and a painting of Priapus weighing his enormous penis. Other erotic scenes are painted in a small room by the kitchen.

The ancient Greek visual arts show that they admired a thin, short penis, terminating in a long pointed foreskin; the small

29

penis goes with a scrotum of normal size, while the erect penis is depicted with normal proportions.

Greek artists often emphasised the small pointed penis of Herakles as opposed to the stubby and circumcised genitals of barbarian attendants. Aristotle's explanation for this predilection for small genitals was that the small penis is more fertile than the large one, because the seed has a shorter distance to travel through it, and so doesn't cool off so much.

The Greek taste for dainty, pointed penises led to a custom of infibulation — to prevent the foreskin from becoming damaged while exercising in the nude, young athletes tied it down over the glans with a leather string, sometimes tucking up the penis with the same string as well. The knot was called 'kynodesme' or 'dog tie', and functioned something like a jock strap.

One Greek vase shows a musician, whose hands are fully occupied with the double pipe, having a spontaneous ejaculation, while a bewildered bee dodges the bombardment.

There is also an ancient Greek depiction of a hairy satyr masturbating while pushing a penis-substitute into his own anus.

Egypt's king Menaphta, who defeated the Libyans in 1300 BC, collected the penises of his slain enemies as battle trophies.

During the summer of 415 BC, Athens was shaken by a scandal. A group of conspirators, moving through the city under cover of night, mutilated the 'herms', statues of the god Hermes — these statues were plain rectangular pillars, with a head and erect male genitals. Almost all of them were castrated — a highly symbolic crime. There were hundreds of them, in private and public places. It was never discovered who did the terrible deed. (30)

In ancient Greek comedy there are a number of jokes about the use, by women of a respectable class, of self-satisfiers or dildos, made of leather. They were known as *olisboi*, derived from a verb meaning to glide or slip. A few vases show naked women using them in fairly fantastic ways — they could be prostitutes, or simply imaginary scenes.

The island of Lesbos, to the ancient Greeks, was not associated with female homoerotism but with fellatio — the verbs '*lesbiazo*' and '*lesbizo*' refer to that practice. The ancient Greek word for 'lesbian woman' in our sense was '*tribas*', from a root meaning 'rub'.

In an old Greek comedy, one woman suggests that the dildo resembles the real organ as the moon resembles the sun it looks the same but lacks heat. (**31**)

FEMALE BITS AND HOW TO USE THEM

In the Moche pottery of prehistoric Peru, males sometimes caress women's chins, and occasionally touch their breasts, but there are no cases of these being sucked or kissed. In fact, kissing of any kind is only depicted between women and corpses.

The Egyptians used the word for female private parts as a deprecation a woman who had played a dirty trick on someone was called a 'kat tahut' — 'kat' means vulva, while 'tahut' probably means prostitute. Vulvas were carved on pillars to call people cowards.

The Egyptians were very amused by female flashers one tomb inscription tells the story of Re, chairman of the council of gods, who was sulking after being insulted by a rival. He only cheered up after his daughter Hathor lifted up her skirt towards him; this made him laugh uncontrollably, and he went back to work on the council.

In the emperor Nero's reign, see-through clothes were all the rage in Rome, exposing breasts and genitals. Seneca, the first century philosopher, noted that this meant women had nothing left to reveal to their lovers in the bedroom that they had not already shown on the street.

Remote Easter Island, in the South Pacific, has many amazing rock-carvings of vulvas. The clitoris was deliberately lengthened from an early age, and girls were expected to straddle two rocks to display them to priests at certain ceremonies at Orongo, a clifftop ceremonial site. The longest were honoured by being immortalised in stone, and their proud owners would get the best warriors as husbands. These littoral clitoral displays thus led to artists beavering away at images of the island's finest.

Women in Classical Athens removed their pubic hair by singeing and plucking.

NUMBER ONES AND
NUMBER TWOS

Captain John G. Bourke's book of 1891, *Scatalogic Rites of all Nations*, was marked 'Not for General Perusal'. Among the 'disgusting rites' covered is one he witnessed among the Zuni of New Mexico in 1881 — the Urine Dance. During a parody of a Catholic service, some men drank heartily from a vessel of urine. More was then brought, a large tin pailful, not less than two gallons.

> The dancers swallowed great draughts, smacked their lips and, amid, the roaring merriment of the spectators, remarked that it was very, very good ....
> one expressed regret that the dance had not been held out of doors, in one of the plazas ... there they always made it a point of honor to eat the excrement of men and dogs.

As for the Celtiberians of Spain, although they boasted of cleanliness both in their nourishment and in their dress, it was not unusual for them to wash their teeth and bodies in urine. Strabo said that the Iberians:

> do not attend to ease or luxury, unless one considers it can add to the happiness of their lives to wash themselves and their wives in stale urine kept in tanks, and to rinse their teeth with it, which they say is the custom both with the Cantabrians and their neighbours.

Cosmetics: Pliny claimed that pigeon's dung was applied externally for all spots and blemishes on the face, as was crocodile dung, which also removed freckles. 'An application of bull-dung, they say, will impart a rosy tint to the cheeks, and not even crocodilea is better for the purpose'. Galen and Dioskorides also alluded to the extensive use, by Greek and Roman ladies, of crocodile dung as a cosmetic, while Sextus Placitus said bull-dung was used by women to remove all facial blemishes. Paullini said that human excrements have peculiar salts that are more strengthening and useful than soap, so a young girl could improve her complexion wonderfully by washing her face in cow-dung, and drinking her brother's urine fresh and warm, while fasting. The urine of a boy took away freckles from a face washed with it, while the crust that gathers on urine standing in chamber pots should be rubbed on birth-marks on children. Dog urine was prescribed to restore the colour of the hair.

According to Pliny, the Scythians preferred mares for the purposes of war because they can pass their urine without stopping in their career.

Early travellers among the Chukchi of Siberia reported that they offered their women to the travellers, but the latter had to show themselves worthy by undergoing a disgusting ordeal — the girl or woman who was to spend the night with the guest presented him with a cup of her urine, and he had to rinse his mouth with it. If he was brave enough to do this, he was considered a sincere friend; if not, an an enemy of the family.

The Chukchi used to pretend to be passing urine in order to catch their animals which they wanted to use with their sleds. The reindeer, horses and cattle of the Siberian tribes are very fond of urine, probably because of the salt it contains, and when they see a man walking out from the hut, as if for the purpose of relieving his bladder, they follow him up so closely that he finds the operation anything but pleasant.

The dogs of the Eskimo are equally fond of excrement, especially in cold weather, and when a resident of the Arctic desires to relieve himself, he finds it necessary to take a whip or stick to defend himself against the energy of the hungry dogs. Often, when a man wants to urge his dog-team to greater exertion, he sends his wife or one of the boys to run ahead, and when at a distance, to stoop down and make believe they are

32

relieving themselves. The dogs are thus spurred to furious exertion, and the boy runs on again, to repeat the delusion. This never fails of the desired effect, no matter how often repeated (32).

Divination: The ancient Peruvians had one class of 'wizards' who 'told fortunes by maize and the dung of sheep', while eighth-century Europe also had pagan superstitions involving divination or augury by the dung of horses, cattle or birds.

Among the superstitious practices of the Greeks, Plutarch mentions 'rolling themselves in dung-hills', 'foul expiations', 'vile methods of purgation', 'bemirings at the temple', with 'penitents wrapped up in foul and nasty rags' or 'rolling naked in the mire'.

The Romans and Egyptians had gods of excrement, whose special function was the care of latrines and those who frequented them. According to the eighteenth-century Spanish

author Torquemada, the Egyptians 'used to adore stinking and filthy privies and water-closets .... and they adored the noise and wind of the stomach when it expels from itself any cold or flatulence.' The Romans also venerated latrines, and made sacrifices to them. The Roman goddess was called Cloacina, one of the first of the Roman deities, believed to have been named by Romulus himself. Under her charge were the various cloacae, sewers, privies, etc. There was also a god of ordure named Stercutius; one for other conveniences, Crepitus.

Several seventeenth-century travellers to Tibet reported that the grandees of the kingdom were very anxious to procure the excrements of the Grand Lama, which they usually wore about their necks as relics, in the form of amulets or as powder in bags;

and they mixed his urine with their victuals, imagining this would secure them against all bodily infirmities (**33**).

It was forbidden to commit desecration — the Romans had inscriptions warning of the wrath of the twelve great gods, and Jupiter and Diana too, against all who did any indecency near temples or monuments. The Emperor Caracalla put to death those who urinated in front of his statues.

The Assyrians' Venus had offerings of dung placed upon her altars, while their neighbours, the Israelites and Moabites, had a similar ceremonial in their worship of Bel-phegor (see above, p.62). The devotee presented his naked posterior before the altar and relieved his bowels, making an offering to the idol of the foul emanations. All the outward orifices of the body were presented to the idol, as well as all their emanations or excretions: tears from the eyes, wax from the ears, pus from the nose, saliva from the mouth, and urine and dejecta from the lower openings (**34**).

34

The Mexicans had a goddess, Suchiquecal, the mother of the human race, depicted in a state of humiliation, eating ordure; another goddess, Tlacolquani, was also an eater of ordure because she presided over loves and carnal pleasures, and heard and pardoned the confessions of men and women guilty of unclean and carnal crimes.

Herodotus said that Egyptian women urinated standing up, and men sitting down. They relieved themselves indoors and ate outside. It is said that Apache men also urinated sitting down, but the women did it standing up. The same has also been said of the Mojaves of the Rio Colorado, and of some Australian Aboriginal tribes (**35**).

A genuine Pompeii graffito — *Hac ego cacavi* — I had a shit here (**36**).

35

The HAPPY

CRAPPER HAD A GOOD ONE HERE!

ASSISTANT CLEANERS REQUIRED

36

From ancient Cyprus, a seventh-century BC jug from Karpass, now in the British Museum, shows a ship carrying two large storage jars. A man squats on one of the two steering oars, and defecates towards a large fish.

The Chumash of California had a somewhat dirty 'coyote dance' — the dancer was a single man, impersonating the coyote. He sang 'The devil goes ahead. The tail swishes, so that the hunk of crap remains here on the ground.' During the last part of the song, he was trying to persuade someone to come over to lick his penis for him; but by the last verse, he had lost all hope and so did it himself. The last part of the song meant to swing your tail so that you would be able to defecate, and the dung would remain there for the coral snake. He continued: 'Do not distrust me. All this shit piled high — I have crapped it all'. With the last verse, the coyote licked his penis. Then: 'Do not think me arrogant — Everything that is piled up here is my crap.' As he began to sing this last verse, he loosened his garment, and when finished, he squatted down and defecated amid the people. The dancer took a drink of seawater in the morning so that when this part of the dance came he could crap on cue.

A Javanese rock-shelter near Kadiri, whose decoration dates to the eleventh century AD, shows a story from the Arjunawiwaha. Arjuna is practising asceticism — the gods send down two heavenly nymphs to test his resolve and the strength of his meditation by wrapping themselves around him. He passes the test, and so receives the two nymphs as his wives. For some obscure reason, the carving shows one nymph relieving herself in a stream.

Down to the early fifth century BC, Greek painters sometimes portrayed disgusting subjects on vases: a man wiping his anus, an explosion of diarrhoea at a party, copious drunken vomiting. In one, a squatting youth simultaneously urinates and defecates on the ground, and the painter has made his penis loll to one side lest our view of the faeces be obscured. On another vase, a man reclines on each side, happily masturbating, while under each handle a dog defecates.

Diocles, a Roman charioteer, had one horse that had won over 200 races. This horse, named Passerinus, was so revered that soldiers patrolled the streets when he was sleeping to keep people from making any noise. When a rumour went around that Passerinus had been doped by rivals, people hurried to the stable to taste his dung to see if it were true.

Most Roman charioteers coated themselves with boar's dung in the belief that the odour kept the horses from stepping on a man if he was thrown from his chariot. And the professional chariot-racers of ancient Rome were encouraged to promote muscle-growth by drinking a solution of dried boar's dung (**36**).

Wild animals were on display at the Tower of London in the seventeenth century — one visitor, Ned Ward, wrote of 'a leopard who is grown as cunning as a cross Bedlamite that loves not to be looked at. For as the madman will be apt to salute you with a bowl of chamber-lie, so will the leopard, if you come near him, stare in your face and piss upon you, his urine being as hot as aqua fortis and stinks worse than a polecat's.'

A scene on a Greek potsherd shows a caricature of a shitting man, about to wipe himself with one hand and holding his nose with the other. His circumcised, droopy penis reaches down almost to his heels.

Other Greek vases depict a harlot urinating into a chamber pot; a satyr having sex with a startled-looking doe; older prostitutes being penetrated orally and anally at the same time.

36

AMATEUR PROS

Herodotus says that King Rhampsinitus bade his daughter to sit in a certain room and receive all alike who came; before she had intercourse with any, she should compel him to tell her what was the cleverest trick and the greatest crime of his life — this was so that the king could find a certain thief.

Herodotus also says that King Cheops of Egypt likewise made his daughter sit in a chamber and exact payment. She, they say, doing her father's bidding, was minded to leave some memorial of her own, and demanded of everyone who sought intercourse with her that he should give her one stone to set in her work; and of these stones they built the pyramid that stands midmost of the three, over against the great pyramid; each side of it measures 150 feet (37).

Herodotus also said that the Babylonians have 'the foulest of customs': every woman must once in her life act as a prostitute of Aphrodite and offer herself to a stranger for sex outside the goddess's temple. The ugly ones may have to wait as long as four years before someone takes them up on their offer .... Among the Nasamones of Libya everybody sleeps with the bride at the wedding party. Among other people 'women took pride in having slept with many men, and placed a ring around an ankle for every conquest.

ATTITUDES TO SEX

The Egyptians would call sex 'spending a pleasant hour together', but outside marriage it could be called ' entering a house' (38). If a single word was required, there were twenty to choose from. Very few erotic scenes are known in their art — one tiny little hieroglyph in a tomb of the Middle Kingdom shows a couple intimately linked on top of a bed. This sign has since been erased from the wall, but it was copied by the mid-nineteenth century.

Concubine figurines were important in Egyptian funerary equipment — through magic they came alive in the tomb, excited and strengthened the virility of the tomb owner, and gave him pleasure.

Some think that the notorious Turin papyrus from Thebes, of 1150 BC, depicts the amorous adventure of a priest of Amun and a Theban whore; but in fact it appears to represent a number of different men and women, and is similar to scenes drawn on flakes of limestone or pottery from the workers' village at Deir el-Medina.

Vase paintings show that Greeks practised intercourse in many positions. In their literature, and especially comedy, the positions are named, with many names deriving from traditional wrestling postures.

The late fourth-century Greek historian Theopompus said of the Etruscans:

> It is customary among the Etruscans to share their wives .... to them it is not shameful to be seen in the nude .... so far removed are they from prudery that when the master of the house is making love and someone calls for him, they openly say that he is having such-and-such done to him, shamelessly calling the act by its name.' (39)

CRIME AND PUNISHMENT

Diodorus, a historian of the first century BC, says that if a man violated a married woman, he was emasculated; if it was adultery with consent, the man got a thousand blows with a rod, and the woman had her nose cut off.

An eighth-century Irish 'Table of Commutations' says of sinners who need to hold prayer vigils that they should, in order to stay awake, lie down not only in water, on nettles or on nutshells, but also sometimes with a corpse in the grave.

Among the monks of the early Christian church, homosexuality was euphemistically called a 'special friendship'. Each monastery had its own rules to control the behaviour of the monks, and these featured a variety of physical punishments to deter

HE'S A GONER.
IT DIDN'T WORK!

40

homosexual activity. Usually, any outward display of affection of one man for another was disciplined as severely as the sexual act itself. Even such innocent practices as tucking a tunic around the thighs while laundering clothes was forbidden as a possible source of temptation for another. Nocturnal emissions were also a source of great concern for the monks.

> To explain the uncontrollable dreams that brought such intense pleasure, they invented the succubus, a beautiful female demon who tempted men in their sleep. To ward against her attentions, monks would tie a metal crucifix to their genitals before retiring for the night.

This custom actually originated in the Roman arena, where gladiators tied bits of cold metal to their testicles on the night before a combat — they believed that the metal's chill would prevent them having an involuntary nocturnal ejaculation that would sap their strength (40).

And there is much more from the early Celtic church: for example, Cunmean's Penitential was composed in the seventh century AD and devoted particular attention to homosexual activities between men. It catalogued virtually every potential sexual variation, and the degree of punishment demanded depended on the extent of homosexual contact: passionate kissing earned eight fasts, but a simple kiss only six. Mutual masturbation and interfemoral stimulation received several years of reduced rations. Cunmean reserved the most severe punishment of seven years atonement for anal intercourse.

However, standards seem to have been slightly different for the ladies. As early Irish Christian nuns, the virgins of Kildare shared with their Roman Christian sisters a loathing for sexual relationships with men. But they may not have been completely celibate. Brigid herself (the Abbess of Kildare) shared her bed with Darlughdacha .....on one occasion, Darlughdacha looked lustfully at a passing warrior. To punish and purify her, Brigid made her walk in shoes filled with hot coals. Presumably, Brigid took Darlughdacha back into her bed when she felt the woman had suffered enough for this heterosexual flirtation (41).

42

In ancient Greece, a male adulterer could be punished by having a large radish stuck up his rectum, doubtless symbolizing the penis of the injured husband. As a further insult, the adulterer was subject to having his pubic hair singed off, whereby he was made to look like a woman (**42**).

In the recently excavated Augustinian Friary of Kingston-upon-Hull, in northern England, some coffin burials of 1340–1360, the time of the Black Death, contained monks accompanied by what seem to be flagellation sticks — they are a metre long, and made of willow or hazel to be extra whippy.

In the Brehon law of Celtic society, if a man forcibly shaved the pubic hair of an unwilling woman, he was liable for her full honour-price and a 'dire' (punitive fine) (**43**). On the other hand, a woman could divorce her husband if he were clearly barren, impotent or very fat. 'The Celts believed that extreme

male obesity was a barrier to efficient lovemaking and placed an intolerable burden on the female partner.' Moreover, if a husband revealed his wife's intimate secrets to another, or displayed such sexual desire for other men or boys that his wife was deprived of his conjugal services, she could divorce him.

In medieval London, if butchers were caught selling bad meats ('putrid, rotten, stinking, and abominable to the human race'), the culprits were punished by being placed in the pillory and having the putrid matter burnt beneath their noses.

Torture: The ancient Chinese had a curious and horrible form of punishment. Some criminals were enclosed in barrels or boxes filled with building lime, and exposed in a public street to the rays of the noonday sun; food in plenty was within reach of the unfortunate wretches, but it was salt fish, or other salty foods, with all the water needed to satisfy the thirst this food was certain to excite, but in the very alleviation of which the poor criminals were only adding to the torments that would overtake them when by a more copious discharge from the kidneys the lime would 'quicken' and burn them to death.

THE SHORT, THE TALL
AND THE UGLY

The deformed and disabled in the Graeco-Roman world were regarded as outsiders, made (according to Pliny, the first century AD naturalist) by Nature to amuse herself and create wonder in us. Some turned it to their advantage — in fact, major employment opportunities awaited those willing to perform at parties or in the theatre. Some were credited with magic powers (a large penis was a useful qualification — it was thought to attract the gaze of the Evil Eye away from an intended victim). Others might be 'lucky' enough to be collected by an emperor, a very popular hobby.

Aristocratic Roman names commonly denoted disability — Flaccus (Big ears), Naso (Big nose), Crassus (Fatso), Strabo (Cross-eyed), and Peditus (possibly Farter).

Cicero tells of a midget witness whom Lucius Philippus asked permission to question. 'Be short' said the judge; 'I'll be as short as the witness' quipped Lucius.

At moments of crisis the ugly and deformed, like other marginal groups, often become subject to physical persecution which may result in their death. For example, in ancient Greek society they selected a victim known as a 'pharmakos' or 'scapegoat', upon whom the blame for any evils afflicting the community was laid. The victim, who was often but not invariably ugly and deformed, underwent a ritual expulsion or, far less often, execution. They chose the ugly or deformed because these people were believed to harbour a grudge against Nature or the gods for making them freaks, as well as against society as a whole for denying them their full human status.

One account, based on the sixth-century BC poems of Hipponax, tells:

> The *pharmakos* was in ancient times the expiatory offering as follows. If a misfortune afflicted a city as the result of divine wrath, whether famine or plague or some other catastrophe, they led out the ugliest person of all for sacrifice, to be the expiation and *pharmakos* of the suffering city. When they had arranged for the sacrifice to take place at a suitable spot, they placed cheese, barley meal and dried figs in the hands of the victim. After beating the victim seven times on the penis with squills [onion bulbs] and branches of wild fig and other wild trees, they finally set light to him on a fire consisting of wild branches. Then they cast his ashes to the winds and to the sea, so that this should be an expiation for the suffering city.

Deformed slaves are often mentioned in Latin literature — they were very popular. In fact it seems no fashionable household was complete without a generous sprinkling of dwarfs, mutes, cretins, eunuchs and hunchbacks, whose chief duty seems to have been to undergo degrading and painful humiliation in order to provide amusement at dinner parties and other festive occasions (**44**). The pretentious Zoilus, ridiculed by Martial, was attended by a catamite who supplied him with red feathers to assist him to vomit, as well as by a eunuch who steadied his wavering penis over a chamber pot while he was urinating.....

In one of Martial's epigrams, a guest observes how an adulterous pair use a cretinous slave to pass lascivious kisses slyly back and forth by proxy, under the eyes of the woman's unsuspecting husband:

> Labulla has discovered how to kiss her lover in the presence of her husband. She constantly slobbers over her diminutive cretin. The lover then straightaway grabs hold of him dripping with kisses, and, having filled him up with his own, returns the

cretin to his smiling mistress. How much bigger an imbecile than the cretin is the husband!

Some Romans were actually prepared to pay more for deformed slaves than for physically perfect ones .... another of Martial's epigrams has the speaker claiming that he paid a vast sum for a slave advertised by the dealer as being an idiot, and now demanding his money back because the slave is anything but a fool!

Plutarch says that, in Rome, the demand for freaks was so great that, in addition to the conventional markets where one could purchase run-of-the-mill handsome boys and beautiful girls, there also existed a 'monster market' ....

Pliny even tells of a dealer called Toranius Flaccus who managed to palm off two exceptionally handsome look-alike slaves as twins for 200,000 sesterces in spite of the fact that they came from different parts of the empire and therefore spoke different dialects. When the fraud was exposed, the shrewd Toranius replied that this was precisely why he had charged so much — because, although there was nothing remarkable about fraternal twins looking alike, 'to find such similarity in persons who belonged to different races was something that was beyond price.'

The fad for dwarfs sees to have originated in Pharaonic Egypt where confidential positions were assigned to ugly dwarfs, and the practice became widespread at the court of the Ptolemies, from where it travelled to Rome. According to Aelius Lampridus, the emperor Commodus favoured a certain individual 'whose penis was larger than that of most animals', on whom he ostentatiously bestowed the title of Onos or Donkey in deference to his majestic member. Moreover, at a dinner party he once exhibited two misshapen hunchbacks, who had been smeared in mustard, on a silver platter ....

Phenomenally large penises were in great demand in the Roman world a certain Hostius Quadra, described by Seneca as a *monstrum*, used to cruise round the public baths looking for the man with the largest sexual organ. A glutton for excess, Hostius then underwent sodomy in a room with enlarging mirrors 'in order to take pleasure in the false size of his partner's member by pretending that it was really that big.' It seems the proud possessor of an outsized organ was treated with some respect, as in Martial's epigram: 'If from the baths you hear a round of applause, Maron's giant prick is bound to be the cause.' (**45**)

The emperor Elagabalus (AD 204–22) is even said to have rounded up all those who were endowed with an unusually large sexual organ, presumably for no loftier scientific purpose than that of comparing their respective lengths .... on another occasion he ordered all hernia sufferers to be brought to his baths so that he could have the perverse pleasure of bathing in their company.

Elagabalus possessed so many living deformities that his successor, Alexander Severus, was obliged to dispose of the entire collection, including the palace dwarfs, fearful that their

45

maintenance would exhaust his treasury. 'Male and female dwarfs, imbeciles, and catamites, and all the entertainers and mimes Alexander gave to the public....'

The Roman emperor himself was also often regarded as a monster or prodigy of a kind — this belief that the behaviour of extraordinary individuals can be accounted for in terms of some physical aberration is certainly still with us, as in the case of the entertaining theory that Adolf Hitler only had one ball, as alleged in a popular British wartime song.

Pliny compiled a catalogue of human oddity — about the tallest giants, the shortest dwarfs, record reproductivity, record longevity, etc. He says King Masinissa of Numidia (third century BC) became a father when he was over 86 years old .... Julius Caesar could simultaneously dictate four different letters to four different secretaries.

Aristotle tells us that the largest number of offspring ever produced at a single delivery was five — a feat achieved by one woman on no fewer than four occasions. In a catalogue of

46

persons of exceptional emaciation, the third-century AD Greek writer Athenaios claims that the poet and grammarian Philetas of Kos, tutor to an Egyptian king, was so thin that he had to wear leaden balls on his feet to prevent the wind from blowing him away (**46**). Capitolinus, a Roman historian of the fourth century AD, reports that the Emperor Maximinus, who is said to have been $8\frac{1}{2}$ft tall, was so strong that 'he could drag wagons with his hands, shift a laden cart unassisted, knock out a horse's teeth with his fist, or break its legs with his heel, crumble tufa, and split saplings. His thumb was so big that he used his wife's

47

bracelet for a ring. His predecessor Elagabulus once mocked him, saying 'You are said to have tired sixteen, twenty, even thirty soldiers at a time. Can you perform thirty times with a woman?'

The record for intercourse with the greatest number of partners over a twenty-four hour period was held by Claudius' wife Messalina, whose total of 25, sarcastically described by Pliny as a 'royal triumph', beat the record of the reigning champion, a notorious prostitute (**47**).

For Roman shows and games, dwarfs often paraded, dressed in extravagant costumes, many with huge, brightly coloured phalli strapped to their loins. They ran about tumbling, doing handstands, and performing simple acrobatic tricks. Sometimes there was a fight between women and dwarfs — as Statius (the first-century AD Roman poet) wrote, 'It was enough to make Mars and the Goddess of Bravery split their sides laughing to see them hacking each other.'

LOOSE WOMEN

At the Roman games, women sometimes broke into hysterical spasms — or had orgasms — and not only the commoners in the upper tiers. When one handsome young gladiator, until recently a farmboy from the Apennines, was paraded before the podium with his bloody sword upraised, a great lady screamed uncontrollably and flung her brooch and necklace into the arena. Then she stripped off her rings, threw them onto the sand, and finally ripped off her undergarments and threw them also. When he encountered the crumpled garments, he thought the lady had simply thrown him her scarf or cloak. As he picked up the clothing to toss it back, the underwear unfolded. The simple boy stood gazing horrified at what he was holding. Then he dropped the garments and fled from the arena 'more terrified of a woman's underwear than he had been of his enemy's sword.' The crowd thought this was killingly funny and nearly died laughing. The patrician lady's husband, however, was not amused (**48**).

Hippla was a noble lady who left her husband and children and fled to Egypt with a gladiator named Sergius. As Juvenal, the first century poet, says, 'Sergius was maimed, getting old, had a battered face, his forehead was covered with welts from his helmet, his nose was broken and his eyes were bloodshot. But he was a swordsman!' Many great ladies enjoyed the company of famous gladiators in their private apartments. At Pompeii, a series of crude sleeping rooms were discovered which turned out to be a gladiators' dormitory; and there, frozen in time, was a gladiator who was holding in his arms, and no doubt protecting her from the hot ashes, an upper-class woman still wearing her jewels.

LECHERS

In later life, the Roman emperor Augustus was a womanizer, and as an elderly man he is said to have still harboured a passion for deflowering girls — who were collected for him from every quarter, even by his wife!

The Roman emperor Caligula used to invite a selection of married women to dinner with their husbands; he would slowly and carefully examine each in turn; then, whenever he felt so inclined, he would send for whoever pleased him best, and leave the banquet in her company. Later he would return, showing obvious signs of what he had been doing, and openly discuss his bedfellow in detail, dwelling on her good and bad physical points, and criticizing her sexual performance.

The Roman emperor Domitian was extremely lustful, calling his sexual activities 'bed-wrestling', like a sport. He preferred to depilate his concubines himself and would go swimming with the commonest of prostitutes.

CESSPITS AND LATRINES

In ancient Rome, there were public latrines, but no privies attached to houses. There were basins and tubs, which were emptied daily by servants detailed for the purpose. No closet-paper was in use, none having yet been invented or introduced in Europe, but in each public latrine there was a bucket filled with salt water and a stick having a sponge tied to one end, with which the passer-by cleansed his person, and then replaced the stick in the tub (49). Seneca describes the suicide of one barbarian captive, a German slave, who rammed one of these sticks down his throat.

49

In the thirteenth century, a Roman bandit Matteo Orsini had the electing cardinals locked up in a small, ruined temple, with no food or water. His soldiers were instructed to urinate and empty their bowels on their Eminences through the holes in the roof until they agreed to nominate the candidate of his choice. But it made conditions so bad in the temple that the new Pope and two of the cardinals died two days after the election.

Before 'garderobes' were built corbelled out from castle walls, they were within the thickness of the walls, so that the filth flowed down the outer face of the building into the moat! The King's privy chamber at Westminster was built on an arch over the water of the Thames — in 1238 the clerk-of-the works was ordered to bar the entrance to this arch with strong iron bars so that no one could enter there!

The records exist of one Henry Ivory, a privy cleaner of fourteenth-century London — he was paid by the number of pipes (one pipe = four barrels) of filth taken away. For 31 pipes he got 51 shillings and 8 pence. The work was probably done at night, with the filth carted to the river where the dung-boats took it away (**50**). In 1281, the cloaca of Newgate Jail had to be cleaned and repaired — thirteen men worked for five nights, cleaning the cesspool, and a breach was made in the stone wall for the filth to be taken out. Four watchmen, hired for four nights, stood at the gap in the wall to prevent prisoners escaping!

In ancient times, the belief was once widely diffused of the power possessed by sorcerers over the unfortunate wretches whose excreta, solid or liquid, fell into their hands. So some scholars think the introduction of latrines and urinals was not for purely hygienic considerations, but also to prevent one's being open to sorcery by these means.

According to Captain Cook, while the New Zealanders had privies to every three or four of their houses, there were none in Madrid until 1760 — the determination of the Spanish king to introduce them and sewers, and to prohibit the throwing of human ordure out of windows after nightfall, as had been the custom, nearly precipitated a revolution (**51**).

Some public cesspools were so big that, when they were cleaned out, they filled 100-120 barrels. The bodies of murdered people were sometimes thrown into these deep wells, because they took several years to be filled, and by the time they were cleaned out the murderer was long gone.

Until the nineteenth century, people often preferred the cool, sparkling waters of city wells to the piped water of the city companies; but the very sparkle of the waters was due to the presence of ammonia and other organic matter in solution — much of this contamination was caused by the frequent pollution of wells by privy filth, and led to outbreaks of cholera and fevers.

The oldest toilet in Japan is of the late seventh century AD, found in 1992 at the Fujiwara Palace site in Nara — it was filled with black mud and *mokkan*, inked wooden tablets used to

record various transactions in the bureaucratic state. There were also lots of fruit seeds, and numerous parasite eggs.

The famous dispute between King Richard the Lionheart and the Arch-Duke of Austria, which led to the English monarch being incarcerated in a dungeon, arose from the insult caused when Richard threw the Austrian standard, the Duke's banner, down a privy.

In medieval London, a ditch in Holborn, next to the inn of the Bishop of Lincoln, was blocked with the entrails of animals, dung, dead dogs, and other putrefying matter. The city moat itself was called Houndsditch because it had often been used as a dumping place for dead dogs!

GRAFFITI

From the Roman world, there are also lead sling-bullets with things like 'Get Pompey' written on them, rather like the 'love to Saddam' that has been chalked on laser-guided bombs in recent years (**52**).

The graffiti of Pompeii include soldiers and gladiators boasting about their love-lives; there is material about gay sex at the palaestra; there are curses, such as: 'May your ulcerous pustules

52

HOW DOES THIS BRIEF ANATOMICAL DESCRIPTION OF CLEOPATRA GRAB YOU?

burst open and burn like never before' (**53**); and Herculaneum has a graffito by a doctor (?) who wrote 'I had a really good crap here'. Pompeii also has drawings with written graffiti — such as *Fortunata (fellat)*.

Deep inside the Ice Age decorated cave of Niaux, France, there is a graffito from a century or two ago saying 'Here at the age of 13 I lost my virginity'. (**54**)

UNDERPANTS

A letter found at Vindolanda fort, near Hadrian's Wall, sent by a mother to her (doubtless shivering and grateful) soldier son, says 'I have sent you ... woollen socks .... two pairs of sandals and two pairs of underpants.'

It seems the Bronze Age boat found at Dover a few years ago was once saved from sinking by having someone's underpants shoved in the hole — the ultimate sacrifice.

The excavation of Kingston-upon-Hull's Augustinian Friary unearthed the shroud burials of six men of 1410-30 who were fashion victims — they were all wearing 'boxer shorts', underpants of good-quality wool. This was a new fashion, brought about by the adoption of canvas breeches, which chafed terribly — hence these underpants 'for chaps'.

54

PHILTRE TIPS

An Egyptian papyrus in the British Museum provides the recipe for a love potion to win a woman's love: the man has to mix some dandruff from a murdered person's scalp with some barley grains and apple pips, then add a little of his own blood and semen, and finally the blood of a tick from a black dog. This mixture, if slipped into the woman's drink. should have devastating consequences (**55**). Another winning formula, designed to make a woman enjoy love-making, was to rub the foam from a stallion's mouth into one's member.

A Chinese manual on camel husbandry of the twelfth century says that if your camel suffers from violent wind, the remedy includes 'powder of centipedes, beans soaked in wine, acupuncture behind the ears, and the letting of a great quantity of blood.'

Various formulas have come down to us from the Classical world for love philters, and cures for them, involving human excrement, perspiration, menses or semen. Human ordure, in particular, was in constant use in the manufacture of these philters, being administered both internally and externally. It was sometimes put in porridge, and in other cases in shoes — for example, a man who made such use of the excrement of his lady love was completely cured of his infatuation, after wearing the defiled shoes for one hour.

Pliny claimed that the urine that has been voided by a bull immediately after covering, taken as a drink, was an aphrodisiac; another was to rub the groin well with earth moistened with this urine. An ointment of the gall of goats, incense, goat-dung and nettle-seeds was applied to the privy parts before copulation, to increase the amorousness of women. And, according to Pliny, 'They say that if a man takes a frog, transfixes it with a reed

entering its body at the sexual parts, and coming out at the mouth, and then dips the reed in the menstrual discharge of his wife, she will be sure to conceive an aversion for all paramours.'

Philters made with menstrual and a hare's blood drove the recipient to mania and suicide, but could also be used to make people impenetrable to an enemy's weapon and to cure burning sores.

Many believed that the 'magnetic power' of human seed could be used in philters, and that by it a lover could feed the flame of his mistress's affections; it was prepared from what was known as 'magnetic mummy', which, being given to a woman, threw her into an inextinguishable frenzy of love for the man or animal yielding it.

Chinese emperors were required to keep 121 wives (the number was thought to have magical properties), and make love to 10 every night. A Taoist manual advised that this could be made possible by applying sheep's eyelid marinaded in hot tea to the imperial penis (56).

Where anti-philtres are concerned, Pliny claimed that mouse-dung, applied in the form of a liniment, acts as an antiphrodisiac; and that a lizard, drowned in urine, has the effect of an antiphrodisiac upon the man whose urine it is. The same property is to be attributed to the excrement of snails and pigeon's dung, taken with oil and wine. He also wrote that 'a woman will forget her former love by taking a he-goat's urine in drink.' Hen-dung was an antidote against philtres, especially those made of menstrual blood; dove-dung was also used for the same purpose, but was less efficacious.

According to Paullini,'a man was given in his food some of the dried ordure of a woman he formerly loved, and that created a terrible antipathy toward her.' Hardly surprising, surely?

But to break up a love affair, nothing was superior to the simple charm of placing some of the ordure of the person seeking to break away from love's thrall in the shoe of the one still faithful, as described above — though Pliny also claimed that 'If a man makes water upon a dog's urine, he will become disinclined to copulation.' Shoes could also be used in other ways — if a man, who under the influence of a philtre was forced to love a girl against his will, would put on a pair of new shoes, and wear them out by walking in them, and then drink wine out of the right shoe, where it could mingle with the perspiration already there, he would promptly be cured of his love, and hate take its place.

Roman magicians, according to Pliny, asserted that 'the heart of a horned owl applied to the left breast of a woman, while asleep, will make her disclose all her secret thoughts.'

UNDER DOCTOR'S ORDURES

Pliny claimed that seminal fluid was a sovereign remedy for the sting of a scorpion. Male urine cured gout, and urine also cured eruptions on the bodies of infants, corrosive sores, running ulcers, chaps upon the body, stings inflicted by serpents, ulcers of the head, and cancerous sores of the generative organs .... Every person's urine is the best for his own case.

Pliny also gives a huge list of remedies involving the dung of different animals and birds (57). For example, badger-dung, cuckoo-dung and swallow-dung, taken internally, cure the bite of a mad dog; cat-dung, rubbed on the neck, removes bones from the throat; poultry-dung — but only the white part — is an excellent antidote to the poison of fungi and mushrooms; it is also a cure for flatulence and suffocations, which is bizarre since if any living creature only tastes this dung, it is immediately attacked with griping pains and flatulence. Ashes of mouse-dung, raven-dung and sparrow-dung were plugged into carious teeth, and used externally for all tooth troubles. Mouse-dung was good for imparting sweetness to sour breath, while pigeon-dung was used as a gargle for sore throats. Moose-dung, used externally, was good for swelled breasts.

Dioskorides also had lots of tips involving dung — for instance, crocodile dung was in high repute as a cosmetic, though purchasers were warned that it was frequently adulterated with the excrement of starlings fed on rice.

Sextus Placitus, a fourth century AD author, claimed that the urine of a virgin boy or girl was an invaluable application for affections of the eyes; also for stings of bees, wasps and other insects. As a cure for elephantiasis, the urine of boys was to be drunk freely, while the crust from human urine was useful in burns and in bites of mad dogs.

Paracelsus, a sixteenth century alchemist, wrote:

> the olde Physitians made very many medicines of
> most filthy things, as of the filth of the eares, sweat
> of the body, of women's menstrues, of the Dung of
> man and other beastes, spittle, urine, flies, mice, the
> ashes of an owle's head, etc......I call to mind a
> storie...of Herachio Ephesio, which being sick of a
> leprosie, despising the help of Physitians, anoynting
> himself over with cow-dung, set himselfe in the sun
> to drie, and falling asleepe was torn to pieces by
> dogges (**58**).

Other remedies listed by Pliny involved ear-wax; woman's milk,
especially of a woman who had just borne male twins ('if a
person is rubbed at the same time with the milk of both mother

JUST AS WELL THE DOGS GOT HIM.
HE WASN'T USING FACTOR 33
COW DUNG!

58

and daughter, he will be proof for all the rest of his life against all affections of the eyes; mixed with the urine of a youth who has not yet arrived at puberty, it removes ringing in the ears'); human sweat (if the perspiration of a fever-stricken patient was mixed with dough , baked into bread and given to a dog, the dog would catch the fever and the man recover); tartar (impurities from the teeth and the dirt from soiled stockings were a remedy for nose-bleed); and human blood — Faustina, the wife of the emperor Marcus Aurelius, was anxious to have a child, so she drank the warm blood of a dying gladiator, and then shared her husband's bed — she at once became pregnant and brought forth the cruel Commodus; epileptics would sometimes drink a draught of the warm blood caught gushing from the neck of a decapitated criminal.

Human flesh, from corpses, was administered under the name 'Mummy'; it was preferably from a malefactor, hanged on a gibbet, never buried, and the age should be between 25 and 40, of good constitution, without organic or other diseases, and gathered in clear weather.

In ancient Egypt, the use of contraceptives was known: one of the earliest methods, described in the Kahun papyrus, was to mix crocodile dung into a paste, which was made into a sort of tampon and inserted into the vagina. Another was to make a kind of tampon with honey, which is indeed a mild spermicide.

King Pyrrhos of Epiros had a big toe which was allegedly capable of curing diseases of the spleen when rubbed on the infected area. .... His toe did not burn when the rest of his body was cremated.

Sahagún gives details of how the ancient Mexican formula for eradicating dandruff. It began by cutting the hair close to the root, and washing the head well with urine... Hippocrates recommended dove-dung, applied externally, in the treatment of baldness. Pliny claimed that the urine of the foal of an ass would thicken the hair, while camel dung, reduced to ashes and mixed with oil, would curl and frizzle the hair.

Human seed was often employed as medicine. Some credited it with a wonderful efficacy in relieving inveterate epilepsy, or restoring virility impaired by incantation or witchcraft; for which purpose it was used while still fresh, before exposure to the air, in pottage. The Albigensians or Cathars of medieval France are alleged to have sprinkled human semen on the eucharistic bread, possibly with the idea that the bread of life should be sprinkled with life-giving excretion.

Nature's Viagra: For impotence and loss of virility, Paullini recommends drinking the urine of a bull, immediately after he has covered a cow, and smearing the pubis with the bull's excrements; and also to piss through the engagement ring. Another cure for this infirmity was that the bridegroom should catch a fish, forcibly open its mouth, urinate into it, and then throw the fish back in the water, upstream; then try to copulate, taking care to urinate through the wedding ring, both before and after.

For sterility, Pliny recommends the application of a pessary made of the fresh excrement voided by an infant at the moment of its birth, while the urine of eunuchs was considered to be highly beneficial as a promoter of fruitfulness in females. Hawk-dung, drunk by a woman before coitus, insured conception; and goose or fox dung rubbed upon the pudenda of a woman aided in bringing about conception. But such remedies needed to be used with care — one woman applied the dung of a wolf to her private parts, and soon after bearing a child found him possessed of a wolfish appetite!

Dioskorides prescribed both human ordure and the dung of the vulture to bring about the expulsion of the foetus, and Pliny prescribed goose dung for this purpose; but according to Avicenna, the dung of the elephant or menstrual blood prevented conception.

Finally, Pliny cites the method of curing a bad cough by spitting into the mouth of a toad (**59**).

59

A FINAL NOSEGAY

In ancient Athens, when the bride arrived at the groom's house, a basket of nuts was poured over her head for good luck by the other women of the household, a treatment also extended to newly purchased slaves. This was called the '*katachysmata*' or 'downpourings'.

A genuine Egyptian curse: 'Anyone who does anything bad to my tomb, then the crocodile, the hippopotamus and the lion will eat him.'

In 1356, Abbot John of Kirkstall Abbey, at Leeds in northern England, organized some of his monks and four laymen into a gang to terrorize the neighbourhood. They besieged houses, damaged property, and stole goods!

The Egyptians hired female mourners to accompany the deceased to the last resting place — they covered their hair with ashes and wept and wailed on the tomb. In Egypt, it is said that in whatever house a cat died all the family shaved the eyebrows.

The Epic of Gilgamesh of 3000 BC, the world's first written story, begins with the gods creating a wildman, Enkidu, to divert King Gilgamesh from his habit of demanding first sexual congress with the local brides. Enkidu got his own sexual education from a rural prostitute: 'For six days and seven nights Enkidu was erect' before he was ready to fight Gilgamesh.

In Aristophanes '*The Peace*', Trygaios instructs his slave to throw some barley into the audience (the Greek word for barley, *krithe*, also means penis). The slave reports the job accomplished: 'Of all the spectators present, there isn't one who did not get any barley'. Trygaios: 'The women didn't get any'. Slave: 'But the men will give them some tonight'.

The Romans even exhibited African porcupines in the arena — naked boys had to catch them with their bare hands.

Julius Caesar was something of a dandy, always keeping his head carefully trimmed and shaved; and he was accused of having certain other hairy parts of his body depilated with tweezers. His baldness was a disfigurement which his enemies harped upon, much to his exasperation; he used to comb the thin strands forward, and loved to wear a laurel wreath whenever possible.

No one was allowed to leave the theatre during the emperor Nero's recitals, however pressing the reason, and the gates were kept barred. We read of women in the audience giving birth, and of men being so bored with the music and the applause that they

furtively dropped down from the wall at the rear, or played dead and were carried away for burial (**60**).

The entire body of the Roman emperor Otho (AD 69) had been depilated, and a well-made toupee covered his practically bald head. Since boyhood he had always used a poultice of moist bread to retard the growth of his beard.

The emperor Vespasian always wore a strained expression on his face; once he asked a well-known wit who always used to make jokes about people 'why not make one about me?', and the wit replied 'I will, when you have at last finished relieving yourself.'

The Chinese emperor Cang Wu Wang (473–76) was a juvenile delinquent whose downfall was caused by shooting blunt arrows at a target he had painted on a sleeping minister's belly. The minister retaliated by having him murdered and replaced by his 13-year-old half-brother.

The emperor Jing Zong (824–27) was a reckless teenager who filled the court with religious quacks and alchemists, and shot scented paper darts at his favourite concubines. He was murdered by exasperated eunuchs.

Much scatology and depicting of genitalia appeared in the medieval art and literature and performances of Europe. For example, professional poets in Wales often composed works on sexual topics. In the fourteenth century, Dafydd ap Gwilym composed a poem in which he not only boasts about the size and energy of his penis (described metaphorically as a 'pestle' and an 'expanding gun') but berates it for having a will of its own ('pod of lewdness, door-nail which causes a lawsuit and trouble'). (**61**) More than a century later, poetess Gwerful Mechain composed ·a piece praising female genitals, referring to the vulva as 'a valley longer than a spoon or a hand'. Such works were performed in the halls of their patrons, the gentry. In medieval Ireland, stone carvings known as Sheela-na-gigs — grim-faced women with exaggerated and prominently-displayed genitalia — were often found above or beside doorways and windows, on castles and churches.

In the Classical world, doctors could treat hypospadias, a condition in which male organs suddenly appear on a female. Diodorus records such a case, describing the surgical tidying-up that rendered the organ feasible. The 'wife' ended up renaming herself and joined the army, while the husband committed suicide.

Pre-Christian sexual attitudes persisted in the early Church. Male bishops and abbots practised the custom of cupping their genitals with their hand to affirm an oath. They swore by the sacred seed within them that their words were true and correct (**62**).

Celtic saints were often born from unusual sexual circumstances. Creda was the mother of St Báithín, the second abbot of Iona. She was a good and holy woman who frequently washed her hands and face in a small pool outside a church. One day, a thief hid in a tree over her head. Overcome by her fair face

62

and shapely form, he secretly masturbated, allowing his semen to fall onto a bed of watercress. Perhaps intentionally, perhaps accidentally, Creda ate the watercress and miraculously gave birth to Báithin. This allowed Creda to remain technically virginal while granting Christian sanction to the Celtic belief in orally induced reproduction under wondrous circumstances ....

St Beuno's elderly parents had not indulged in sex for twelve years when his mother amazingly found herself pregnant ....

The greatest insult: The historian Josephus tells us that:

> When the multitude had come to Jerusalem, to the feast of unleavened bread, and the Roman cohort stood over the temple, one of the soldiers pulled back his garment, and stooping down after an indecent manner, turned his posterior to the Jews, and spake such words as might be expected upon such a posture

A riot followed, and ten thousand people were killed (**63**).

Sir Flinders Petrie, the British Egyptologist, took to working in Egypt in flesh-coloured combinations, so that Victorian lady-tourists, who were becoming a problem, would be confronted by what appeared to be a naked man emerging from the tombs, and head straight back to their houseboats and an early tea (**64**).

INDEX